Prophetic Proclamations

Activating the Spiritual Realm to Operate in Your Favor

Kathy DeGraw

KATHY DEGRAW MINISTRIES

Copyright © 2019 Kathy DeGraw

Declarations written by Kathy DeGraw
Published by K Publishing

Cover design by:
Emcat Designs
Facebook: Emcat Designs
Email: Megparker1990@gmail.com

Table of Contents

Introduction

We've all heard about the power of positive thinking, but what about positive speaking. The Bible instructs us in many different passages about our words. Prayer, when spoken out loud into the atmosphere, has powerful results. Jesus spoke out many things, and He experienced nature, people, sickness, and demons responding to what He spoke out.

Now is the time for us to speak out and have things in the natural react to what we have spoken out in the spiritual. This book is to get you to prophetically declare positive things over your life and to have you writing your own prophetic proclamations.

In this book, I have provided prophetic proclamations in which you can declare out loud and call forth those things that do not exist in the natural. By speaking them out into the atmosphere, you will discover your faith will increase, and your circumstances will change.

I also want to empower you to write your own proclamations for situations that need attention in your life. I have included a set of blank pages behind each section of declarations. These blank pages start with thought-provoking questions in order to assist you in writing your own declaration. I have also included blank pages in order for you to use your discernment or allow the Holy Spirit to speak to you.

I have written two additional books on declaring and audible prayer. My book *SPEAK OUT* teaches you the power of declaring through prayer. It will teach you scripturally how Jesus and the Father declared, break down legalistic thoughts and increase your faith for declaring. In this book, I have outlined the proper order of declaring and different ways to write a declaration. I also have a book titled *Warfare Declarations* in which I have written several spiritual warfare declarations for you to use in your prayer time. I invite you to check those resources out on my website at www.kathydegrawministries.org or Amazon.com.

I hope you will enjoy this book and journal. It was my intentions to give you enough space to write your own declarations so that you could declare what the Holy Spirit has given you through my writings and add your own for your convenience of taking it with you as your travel, go to a worship event or walk around your home declaring and proclaiming into the spiritual atmosphere.

May you be abundantly blessed with all knowledge through our Lord, and may the Holy Spirit co-labor with you as you write your own proclamations!

– Kathy

How to Make Your Prayers More Powerful

Jesus made prayer a priority for his life. We read that Jesus spoke to things such as the fig tree (Matt. 21:19), the little girl, saying, "Arise" (Mark 5:41), and He said to the storm, "Peace be still" (Mark 4:39, MEV). When Jesus spoke, people, sickness and disease, nature, and the demonic responded in obedience. Storms ceased; trees withered; and sickness, disease, and demons left.

Are we praying as Jesus did? Why are we, as Christians, not seeing our prayers answered? Jesus has given us that same authority (Luke 10:19). Power went forth as Jesus spoke. When He died and was resurrected, He transferred that power and authority to us. It is similar to having power of attorney over someone. You have authority over their lives and situations. Jesus died and gave us His power of authority. As believers, we need to know that we have the authority to speak to our situations.

Proverbs 18:21 (MEV) reads, "Death and life are in the power of the tongue" and in Matthew, Jesus further talks about faith and speaking out: "So Jesus said to them, 'Because of your unbelief; for assuredly, I say to you, if you have faith as a mustard seed, you will say to this mountain, "Move from here to there," and it will move, and nothing will be impossible for you'"

(Matt. 17:20, MEV). Jesus continually modeled the example of the power of our belief, authority, and the words spoken out of our mouth.

Why are most of our prayers in our minds and not speaking out loud as Jesus did? There is a time to pray in our mind and connect spirit to Spirit with the Father. However, there are times when we need to speak out loud and command the spiritual atmosphere to activate on our words. We need to take authority over the spiritual realm, and that is done by speaking out loud so that the spirit realm can hear what we are commanding it to do, just like Jesus did.

Prophetic Release

I proclaim God's presence, His purpose, and His blessing, to surround me like a shield.

I decree that every prophetic promise scheduled for my life be released and active. I instruct angels to dispatch and release my assignment and destiny. I establish God's will for my life to come forth, with love and power in full manifestation.

I call forth supernatural grace and uncommon favor. Surround me, the righteous, with favor like a shield.

I am blessed, and abundance is forever mine because I serve the poor! The Bible speaks of the blessings of serving the poor, and I receive what the word of God says!

I proclaim God's favor, and that uncommon grace releases upon me and my family. I decree and declare there will be no hindrance or delay to the Word of the Lord over our lives.

I declare the Lord will hasten to perform His Word over my life. No more delay, in Jesus' name.

In my life, family, and ministry, I call forth and establish uncommon favor, uncommon opportunity, and uncommon miracles to manifest.

The Spirit of the Lord is upon me; therefore, I receive and walk-in uncommon grace, unprecedented favor, and an unparalleled anointing.

I manifest God's love, and God displays His agape towards me in supernatural ways.

I declare my prophetic destiny to activate and release. I decree that I experience and implement the God-ordained results that have been planned by the Almighty.

I declare grace, life, and revelation as I stand in the season of open doors. God has set an open door before me that no man can shut. I walk in supernatural favor.

I proclaim that the grace and glory of God overshadow me.

I proclaim that I will experience God's supernatural power and grace. I declare that I am experiencing supernatural opportunities, supernatural visitation, and answered prayers.

Abundance

I command clarity of mind, prophetic vision, and revelation, come forth and activate!

I call forth new hope and speak and declare abundant joy. I decree the heavens are opening on my behalf.

I implore heaven to activate and dispatch angels on assignment to help me accomplish my mission.

I decree this will be a season of change! I declare increase!

I declare my mind will be renewed to believe and receive everything the Lord has for me.

I call forth every good and abundant gift from the Father. He is a God who desires to give good gifts to His children.

I am blessed with every spiritual blessing! The Lord blesses me physically, emotionally, and spiritually.

I am blessed, favored, loved, and wanted! I am called and chosen by God.

I have an eternal inheritance! I am walking in my full destiny.

The prophetic realm is activating on my behalf. The Kingdom of God is manifesting in my favor!

I call forth and declare the abundant flow of heaven. I walk under an open heaven.

I say my year, and my season will increase and release to benefit the Kingdom!

I proclaim this will be a year of the manifestation of my promises. My destiny will unleash, and I will experience supernatural acceleration in the natural and spiritual.

I release angels on assignment to carry out their orders for my family and ministry.

I say I will arise and take my rightful place and position in the Kingdom!

I speak and declare blessings and favor are my portion!

I speak edification, exhortation, and comfort. My words glorify Jesus' name.

I prophesy with my words! My promises and my destiny are coming to pass!

My prophetic words are in fulfillment. Every good and perfect gift is coming my way.

I call these things forth to full activation, in Jesus' name!

I seal it in and declare it is so, in Jesus' name.

Acceptance

God accepts me. I am chosen and accepted by God. I trust and believe the truth of God's word and His great love for me.

I release the need for people's approval. My acceptance and identification are with God.

I will not allow a person's perception of me or rejection displayed towards me to define me.

I carry identification and authority to do spiritual business in the realms of the Spirit. I am powerful and dangerous against the kingdom of darkness.

No one can reject me because God accepts me.

I am loved, chosen, wanted, accepted, and not rejected by the Lord.

Abundance is something we all need to call forth. Where are you lacking? Where do you need to see the abundance of heaven come forth on your behalf? Write your own declaration calling forth what you specifically need in your life.

_____

_____

_____

_____

_____

_____

_____

_____

_____

_____

_____

_____

_____

_____

_____

_____

_____

_____

_____

_____

_____

_____

_____

_____

_____

_____

_____

_____

_____

_____

_____

_____

_____

_____

_____●

No Flesh —
Walking in the Spirit

My flesh is unproductive and unfruitful. I will not submit to the desires of my flesh.

I will walk in the Spirit. I bind and restrict all lust of the flesh.

I bind my mind not to operate in fleshly tendencies.

I proclaim I am teachable and correctable.

I call forth my will to align with God's will.

I command my flesh to submit to my soul, my soul to submit to my spirit, and my spirit to align with the Holy Spirit.

I call forth the spiritual realm and atmosphere to come into alignment with the Word of God and the will of God for my life.

I decree and declare my heart and mind are open to receive from the Lord.

I restrict my flesh from acting out in disobedience. I declare I am disciplined in my soul and spirit.

I bind and restrict my flesh from activating against God's plans for my life.

Faith

I will be in faith and not worry.

I will be in faith and not doubt.

I will be in faith and not fear.

I will be in faith and not concern.

I will be in faith and not fatigue.

I will renew my focus and be in faith.

I will concentrate on God and be in faith.

My mind is disciplined and in faith

My Spirit is strong and in faith.

I live in faith.

Faith manifests through me.

Faith is my portion.

I have an inheritance of faith.

My faith cannot be shaken!

I have supernatural faith!

I decree I have abundant faith! My faith doesn't get stale, dry, or stagnant.

I declare I am a giant in faith!

Faith, not fear, resides in me!

My faith will not be shaken!

My faith is stirred and daily ignited.

My faith is active, moving mountains!

God, I beseech you for a supernatural faith impartation.

Lord, give me more faith!

When declaring, we need to bind our flesh and discover what God's will is for our lives. Take a few moments and journal out God's will for your life and then turn it into a proclamation.

_____

_____

_____

_____

_____

_____

_____

_____

_____

_____

_____

_____

_____

_____

_____

_____

_____

_____

_____

_____

_____

_____

_____

_____

_____

_____

_____

_____

_____

_____

_____

_____

_____

_____

_____•

Faith to manifest your prayers is a necessity if you are going to be calling forth something that you don't see in the natural. In my book *SPEAK OUT*, I discuss how to overcome doubt, unbelief, legalism, and the mindsets you may experience by not being taught about declaring.

Write a declaration based on Scripture and prophetic insights to overcome any faith obstacles and speak it out.

_____

_____

_____

_____

_____

_____

_____

_____

_____

_____

_____

_____

_____

_____

_____

_____

_____

_____

_____

_____

_____

_____

_____

_____

_____

_____

_____

_____

_____

_____

_____

_____

●

_____

Blessings

I declare the blessing of the Lord is upon me.

I am blessed in my coming in and going out!

I call forth the blessings and favor of God and man.

I declare that my blessings are manifesting in abundance!

I call forth every good and perfect gift in my life to manifest now!

I proclaim this is the year for my prophetic words to come to pass, that are according to the will of God and word of God.

I command blessings in my workplace, ministry, and family. Blessings, come forth now!

I say every good thing is coming my way!

I declare all things are working together for my good. I am called according to His purpose.

I speak, and the spiritual realm activates in a positive direction.

I command my angels to be dispatched to bring forth blessings.

I decree every good and perfect gift is being bestowed upon me!

Victory

I claim, command, and decree that I will walk in the authority Jesus has given me. I am a powerhouse for the Kingdom of God.

I proclaim I have been redeemed by the blood of the Lamb. I receive the liberty and freedom He purchased for me.

I accept the atoning work of the cross and speak that it manifests in my life, bringing forth both physical healing and demonic deliverance.

In my life, Lord, may Your name be glorified. In my words, thoughts and actions may Your name Lord be lifted high.

Fear and every fiery dart of the enemy will bow at the feet of Jesus, and since Jesus lives in me, I command fear and every demonic spirit to bow and get out of me, in Jesus' name.

No weapon formed against my mind will prosper, in Jesus' name.

I have the mind of Christ. I have a sound, disciplined, and self-controlled mind.

My mind is steadfast and fixed on You, God, Your ways, and Your Word.

I seal myself and my family into the Sonship of the Kingdom of God.

I decree and declare I am made new in Christ.

I bind, rebuke, and destroy old patterns, habits, and actions.

I destroy familiar spirits in my life. Familiar spirits no longer manifest against me.

I command negative cycles, patterns, and seasons to be gone, in Jesus' name.

I speak and decree I am going up and forward. I declare no more backsliding.

I am anointed. The river of God flows through me!

The glory of the Lord surrounds me!

Miracles, signs, and wonders manifest around me and through me.

I am a new creation in Christ; old things are gone, all things have become new.

I declare my mind is being renewed day by day.

I am a glory carrier.

I am a walking testimony.

I go from glory to glory. The glory of the Lord is my rear guard.

Renewal and Change in a Person

I send forth the fire of the Holy Spirit to convict and expose the enemy.

Convict (insert person's name), Holy Spirit, to seek You.

I proclaim the truth of God's word and their inadequacies to be exposed in their life.

Father, create in (person's name) a clean heart.

Cleanse (_____) and reveal his or her secret faults.

I speak and decree the blinders off their eyes so they may see the truth.

I bind a spirit of pride, control, and offense from activating within them.

I dispatch angels on assignment to (_____).

Put people in their path to influence and speak life into them.

I decree a change in the person I am declaring for and call forth Holy Spirit conviction and obedience, in Jesus' name.

I bind and restrict all demonic activity in them while they are in my presence.

I command no ungodly attachments, defilements, or transferences, in Jesus' name.

I speak and call forth full deliverance and liberation for (_____). Fill them with your love and open their heart to receive from You.

Prophetic Season

I proclaim this is a year of dynamic change and increase for my family.

I declare my assignment will not be interrupted, in Jesus' name.

The blessing that is established for me will come forth!

I put a demand on my prophecies to come forth!

I call forth a new level of faith activation and impartation.

I will have abundant favor and blessing this year.

I decree a year of open doors, expansion in territory, divine contracts, and connections, in Jesus' name.

I speak and decree for demonic attacks and assignments to cease, in Jesus' name.

I proclaim failures and destructions of the past will not manifest again.

I command my full manifestation of blessings to come forth, nothing missing or lacking.

I will walk forward in my full Kingdom inheritance here on earth!

Prayer Increase

I call forth an increase in intercession. Lord Jesus, make my prayers as sweet incense before your throne.

I bind and restrict distractions in my prayer time.

I proclaim my attention will be on you in my prayer time.

I speak and decree that wandering thoughts will not infiltrate and plague my prayer time. Nothing will draw me away from focusing on You and giving You my love, attention, and affections.

I decree and proclaim my prayer life will be fruitful and productive for the Kingdom of God.

I call forth people to arise and be great and mighty prayer warriors.

I proclaim I will be an instrument of prayer.

I decree and declare my prayers will go forth, and no weapon formed against them will prosper.

I call forth a guard of angels to go forth and surround my prayers, executing their orders with precision and accuracy, in Jesus' name..

Divine Strategies

I command divine instructions to come forth. Divine revelation permeates me!

I call forth God's plans and purposes. God gives me the wisdom to complete my tasks!

I proclaim the doors and vaults of heaven are continually open before me!

Words of knowledge come forth in abundance. I lack in nothing I need to operate prophetically.

The wise counsel of the Lord is at my disposal. I have direct communication with my Heavenly Father for instructions and insights.

I have the keys to the Kingdom of heaven. I command those keys to unlock everything that has been hidden and delayed.

I proclaim revelation is in abundance. I do not lack in discernment.

I call forth every hope and dream inside my heart to fully manifest.

I co-labor with the Holy Spirit and angelic realm to manifest God's plans for my life according to His will.

Anointing Increase

I receive the Spirit of revelation and wisdom. Holy Spirit, baptize me in Your fire with the seven functions of the one Holy Spirit, according to Isaiah 11:2.

I declare the Spirit of Wisdom is upon me, releasing divine wisdom into all those I speak.

I say and declare I receive wise counsel, and the Spirit of Counsel, in my secret place time.

I proclaim all the insights I receive are from the Spirit of the Lord. I am not deceived by the adversary's voice.

I declare the Spirit of Might rests upon me, the spirit of power and authority from Jesus.

I speak and believe the Spirit of Fear of the Lord permeates me and arises from within me.

I proclaim the Spirit of Knowledge invades my soul and flows through my veins, bringing the Lord's knowledge into all insights, thoughts, and words spoken.

I speak and declare I have the Spirit of Understanding upon me, understanding, and deep revelation of Your Scripture. The Holy Spirit teaches me, and I receive His insights and wisdom!

Positive proclamations are powerful! The Bible says, "Death and life are in the power of the tongue" (Prov. 18:21). There is power in positive thoughts and words. Write a proclamation establishing over yourself the power of positivity.

_____

_____

_____

_____

_____

_____

_____

_____

_____

_____

_____

_____

_____

_____

_____

_____

The Bible speaks about how we are blessed, and God desires good things for us. Write a proclamation based on Scripture of the blessings the Bible says we can have. If you need help writing a scriptural declaration, refer back to my book, *SPEAK OUT*, where I teach you the three different ways to write a declaration in which one is based on Scripture.

_____

_____

_____

_____

_____

_____

_____

_____

_____

_____

_____

_____

_____

_____

_____

_____

_____

_____

_____

_____

_____

_____

●

_____

People often speak negativity out of their mouths, but as we speak life and positive things, we will feel uplifted and believe what we speak.

Write a positive proclamation that brings out the life in you.

_____

_____

_____

_____

_____

_____

_____

_____

_____

_____

_____

_____

_____

_____

Productivity

I will be in health. I declare by His stripes I am healed.

Healing and wholeness will be mine today because in the Word it says so!

I will have favor in all I do, unexpected favor, supernatural favor, and unprecedented favor.

The Kingdom of God will manifest from me because the Kingdom is within me!

I will get much accomplished today. I bind distractions, delays, and detours, in Jesus' name.

I proclaim my spiritual walk will ignite to a new level today. I will have accelerated growth!

I command no distractions, delays, or detours. My prophetic assignment will go forth unhindered.

I call forth productivity for my day and agenda. God's purposes for my life will go forth!

I invite the Holy Spirit to invade my day. Holy Spirit, you are welcome here! Invade me!

I say the promises of heaven are mine today, in Jesus' name.

I have a Kingdom inheritance. I walk in abundance.

The Word of God manifests in my life!

I decree the will of God will prevail. The abundance of heaven is mine.

Every good and perfect gift comes from above and rains down on me!

All things are working together for my good. I believe it! I receive it!

Dominion

No weapon formed against me will prosper.

I decree that my territory will be expanded.

I will have unprecedented favor in the sight of God and man. Send forth philanthropists and entrepreneurs my way!

I abolish any demonic assignments set against me this day, in Jesus' name, by the blood of the Lamb.

I call forth an abundance of Heavenly rain in my life today and divine appointments. Blessings come forth!

I say the fruit of the Spirit and the gifts of the Spirit will manifest in my life.

I will prosper in all I set my hands to, and God's Word will prosper in my life.

God's plan for my life will prosper, and my prophetic destiny will be set forth into action!

I bind and restrict all demonic, fleshly, and soulish distractions from infiltrating my day.

My day will go forth unhindered. I abolish all warfare attacks and command you to desist from your assignment, in Jesus' name.

I seal this declaration in by the precious blood of the Lamb, in the name of Yeshua Messiah, the Jehovah Nissi, who is the Lord my banner.

.

Daily Shift

I declare and decree a prophetic release over my day, prophecies come forth and be fulfilled.

I release the everlasting, abundant, joy of the Lord into my life today, every day, and always.

I release prosperity, increase, and the abundance of heaven over my life, family, job, ministry, and life.

I render and call forth the heavens to open on my behalf and release every good thing.

I proclaim favor will be my portion today and every day.

I command clarity, focus, and clear vision in my mind for the plans and purposes of God in my life.

I say health, healing, and the blood of Jesus flows through my veins, bringing purity, health, and abundant life.

There will be no contaminants in my soul. I release angels on assignment to reverse and destroy assignments of the enemy.

I call forth my dreams and desires to manifest, in Jesus' name.

This will be a day of focus, accomplishments, and tasks completed.

I call forth productivity today. I abolish all distractions on my day and cover my day in the blood of Christ and dispatch angels to war and activate on my behalf.

I speak and decree there will be no prophetic delays on my assignments.

I say, order, and declare godly phone calls, emails, and messages to come forth, placing a prophetic release and demand on my life and ministry through divine appointments.

I shake loose what is being held up in the spiritual realm against my destiny.

I order angels to go forth on assignment.

In the mighty name of Jesus, I seal this declaration prayer in and call it forth in the precious name of Yeshua Messiah!

Taking authority over the beginning of your day can and will eliminate distractions. When you are focused, you don't need unexpected interruptions. Write a declaration using the facts of the distractions you receive typically and turn the situation around by declaring against them.

_____

_____

_____

_____

_____

_____

_____

_____

_____

_____

_____

_____

_____

The Bible contains many references to rising early and spending time with the Lord the first thing in the morning. Write out how you will spend your mornings and then do it!

_____

_____

_____

_____

_____

_____

_____

_____

_____

_____

_____

_____

_____

_____

_____

_____

_____

_____

_____

_____

_____

_____

_____

_____

_____

_____

_____

_____

_____

_____

_____

_____

_____

_____

_____

_____

●

_____

Home Blessings

I declare the glory of the Lord will reside in my home.

I say and decree the heavens are opened over my household.

In Jesus' name, my home will reside in the peace of Jehovah Shalom, the God of peace.

Yahweh is the Master of my home and family.

The Messiah, the Anointed One, establishes our home.

I proclaim that all the members of my household serve Yeshua.

The glory of the Lord resides within my home; it is full of His presence.

My home is a place where all are welcome to reside and find solace, refuge, and sanctuary.

I speak life to all members of my household and everyone who enters my home; I prophesy to their dry bones, and I say arise and live!

My family stands on the Word of God, and the Word of God goes out of our mouths and lives in all we do.

My family and my home is a temple of the Lord; we are willing vessels ready and able to be used by Him.

As for me and my house, we shall serve the Lord.

My family shall live in unity, love, cooperation, grace, and mercy.

Angels are dispatched to my home and family to guard and protect; they are activated on their assignment!

The blood of Jesus is on my doorposts, windows, entryways, and exits and is applied to my household and family, vehicles, appliances, yard, and property.

I belong to the Lord and therefore, my family belongs to the Kingdom. I call them in and seal them into a right relationship with Jesus.

I call forth the glory of the Lord to saturate my house so people are changed as they enter into His presence in my home. I restrict the enemy from reaping havoc in my home.

Fire of God, permeate my home and family and burn up anything unclean and negative.

I say and proclaim the presence of the Lord resides here.

Every good thing, according to God's will, manifests in my home.

Prophetic words, come forth for those in my family!

I say we shall prosper (succeed) in all we do!

My family shall bear much great fruit!

My family worships the great I AM, the great Lord Jesus Christ!

I call forth this declaration in Jesus' name!

Spouse

Holy Spirit, open the eyes of my spouse to see and know the truth of who I am and the true intentions of my heart.

Holy Spirit, convict my spouse, reveal their sin and inadequacies to them to bring forth change through your correction and direction.

I call forth unity in my home! I proclaim the love of God to saturate us and fill us to overflowing. I declare we will fulfill our calling jointly and individually.

Holy Spirit, convict me to war for my spouse.

I thank You, Lord, that a three-fold cord is not quickly broken and that you are the center of us.

I call forth and proclaim a divine change in my spouse!

I say my family will serve and love the Lord!

I proclaim that my family will be filled with the knowledge of His will in all wisdom and spiritual understanding.

I call forth that my family will walk worthy of the Lord, fully pleasing to Him, being fruitful and faithful in every good work.

I say my family will increase in the knowledge of God and be in obedience and discipline to His word and His will for their lives.

I speak that my family will be strengthened with all might according to His glorious power!

Reflect on the past dissension that has been in your home. Where do you need to be on the offense instead of the defense? Write an offensive declaration to combat the past warfare you have experienced and to call your family, children, or spouse into unity with the word of God.

My thoughts on what I should declare against.

_____

_____

_____

_____

_____

_____

_____

_____

_____

_____

_____

_____

_____

_____

_____ ●

Declaration for my family

_____

_____

_____

_____

_____

_____

_____

_____

_____

_____

_____

_____

_____

_____

_____●

Declaration for my spouse

_____

_____

_____

_____

_____

_____

_____

_____

_____

_____

_____

_____

_____

_____

_____

_____

_____

Declaration for my children

_____

_____

_____

_____

_____

_____

_____

_____

_____

_____

_____

_____

_____

_____

_____

_____

_____

Declaration for my son

_____

_____

_____

_____

_____

_____

_____

_____

_____

_____

_____

_____

_____

_____

_____

_____

_____

_____

Declaration for my daughter

_____

_____

_____

_____

_____

_____

_____

_____

_____

_____

_____

_____

_____

_____

_____

_____

_____

_____

_____

_____

_____

_____

_____

_____

_____

_____

_____

_____

_____

_____

_____

_____

_____

_____

_____

●

_____

Declaration for my daughter

_____

_____

_____

_____

_____

_____

_____

_____

_____

_____

_____

_____

_____

_____

_____

_____

_____

_____

_____

_____

_____

_____

_____

_____

_____

_____

_____

_____

_____

_____

_____

_____

_____

_____

_____

●

_____

Declaration for my daughter

_____

_____

_____

_____

_____

_____

_____

_____

_____

_____

_____

_____

_____

_____

_____

_____

_____

Declaration for my daughter

_____

_____

_____

_____

_____

_____

_____

_____

_____

_____

_____

_____

_____

_____

_____

_____

_____

_____

_____

_____

_____

_____

_____

_____

_____

_____

_____

_____

_____

_____

_____

_____

_____

_____

_____

●

_____

Declaration for myself — what I need to call forth and change.

_____

_____

_____

_____

_____

_____

_____

_____

_____

_____

_____

_____

_____

_____

_____

_____

Divine Release

I will walk in my God-given destiny. I have a solid foundation.

My prophecies are coming forth, speedily, and according to God's will. There are no delays or distractions on my assignment.

I walk in my God-given authority! I rule in dominion!

No weapon formed against me will prosper! No demonic arrow will be fired against me.

I will have life and live it abundantly! I exude the love and joy of Christ!

My life will produce great fruit for the Kingdom! I am fruitful and productive.

God blesses me and shows me great favor. I have unprecedented favor with man.

I walk in prosperity and am rich in the Word! I receive words of knowledge and wisdom.

I have blessings in abundance flowing through me.

I receive prophetic revelation and send it forth. I bless others with prophetic words.

I distribute the love of God to everyone I meet. I am a vessel of His love.

I speak peace from my mouth and encourage others with exhortation, edification, and comfort. My words are prophetic.

Defeat No More!

I am not defeated. I am more than a conqueror in Christ Jesus!

I am empowered from on high! I gain insights from the Lord.

I break agreement with poverty, victim, and defeat mentality, in Jesus' name.

My identity is not in lack, negativity, or as a pauper. I have a royal inheritance.

I am a son of God, and my identity is in Christ. I am a Kingdom citizen.

My mind is renewed, transformed, sound, full of knowledge, and empowered! I am confident, secure, and wise.

My mentality is not dictated by my circumstances. I live by faith, not by sight or emotion.

I command my ungodly soulish tendencies to leave now, in Jesus' name! I will walk in the Spirit, not the flesh.

I am changing behavior and thought patterns for the glory of the Kingdom. I am not a product of my past.

I choose to put on joy and walk in love. I have Christ's characteristics.

I call things forth that are held up in the spiritual realm over my life to manifest that are according to God's will, in Jesus' name.

Mind Declaration

I have a sound mind.

My mind thinks right thoughts.

My mind thinks good thoughts.

My mind is steadfast.

I think on things from above.

I think about positive things.

I have spiritual thoughts.

I have encouraging thoughts.

I have a sound mind.

I have prosperous thoughts.

I take hold of my imagination.

My imagination does not run wild.

Vain imaginations are not in my mind.

I have a sound mind.

My mind belongs to God.

I hold every thought captive.

I bind my mind to the mind of Christ.

Peace runs through my mind.

Worry is a thing of the past.

Fear is non-existent in my mind.

Concern is canceled in my mind.

My mind is right.

It thinks good thoughts.

I have a sound mind.

Peace

I have peace like a river.

It flows through my veins.

It permeates every part of me.

In my path is peace.

Great peace.

There is stillness in my path.

I meditate on God's word.

It brings me peace.

My mouth speaks peace.

My mind thinks about peace.

My body feels peace.

I live in the peace of His presence.

I live in the tabernacle of peace.

This is my confession.

I believe and receive peace.

This is my prophecy over myself.

I believe in peace.

I believe I can have what I say I can have.

I say I have peace.

Peace permeates my soul.

I live in the peaceful river of God.

Peace is mine.

We Suffer from issues such fear, rejection, anger, depression, and other topical issues. As the previous proclamations declared out trust, peace, faith, blessings, and other positive things take a moment and write down what you struggle with and write a declaration against the very thing that has been a stronghold in your life.

My personal declaration to bring me to a place of freedom.

_____

_____

_____

_____

_____

_____

_____

_____

_____

_____

_____

_____

_____

_____

_____

_____

_____

_____

_____

_____

_____

_____

_____

_____

_____

_____

_____

_____

_____

_____

_____

_____

_____

_____●

My Proclamation of joy!

_____

_____

_____

_____

_____

_____

_____

_____

_____

_____

_____

_____

_____

_____

_____

_____

_____●

My Proclamation of perseverance!

_____

_____

_____

_____

_____

_____

_____

_____

_____

_____

_____

_____

_____

_____

_____

_____●

My **Proclamation** for keeping focused and balanced!

_____

_____

_____

_____

_____

_____

_____

_____

_____

_____

_____

_____

_____

_____

_____

_____

_____

_____•

My Proclamation of patience and rest!

_____

_____

_____

_____

_____

_____

_____

_____

_____

_____

_____

_____

_____

_____

_____

●

_____

Kingdom Destiny

I preach to the nations and set people's hearts ablaze for God.

I distribute the fire of God to encourage, inspire, and ignite people to prophesy!

I impact everyone I come in contact with and stir up a hunger and desire in their soul that can't be satisfied.

I have creative ability led by the Holy Spirit's inspiration to lead people to the Lord.

In these last day's I will not be found idle or downtrodden.

The joy of the Lord is my strength, and I have more than enough to accomplish my tasks.

His portion is my inheritance, and I'm taking my inheritance and manifesting the Kingdom out of me here on earth.

There will be no obstructing obstacles to my Kingdom assignment. I bind and restrict enemy assignments and fleshly opposition.

New spiritual positions, elevation, and acceleration are my portion.

I am more than victorious. I am a conqueror. I am developed and equipped for my Kingdom task. I do not lack anything.

I'm released into my assignment, and I'm taking it by force.

I cover it in the blood of Jesus and destroy, abolish, and utterly cut off evil forces set against it, in Jesus' name!

I seal it in and prophesy it to come forth!

Spouse's Ministry Assignment

My spouse will be a strong teacher of the Word.

My spouse will walk in and own with humility, their prophetic destiny.

My spouse will support me in my ministry calling with unity and love.

I proclaim my spouse's anointing is increasing for the glory of God.

I declare my spouse to receive a deeper understanding of the Scriptures.

My spouse will exude love, God's love in each moment, situation, and circumstance.

In my life, my spouse and I will glorify the Father and His Kingdom together.

I call forth ministry assignments for my spouse, separate from me.

Father God, break down their walls, and allow Your love to be received into their heart in Your fullness.

Meeting Atmosphere

I command no weapon formed against these meetings to prosper, in Jesus' name.

I bind any and all demonic influence which has been sent to interrupt this meeting, in Jesus' name.

I say that our prayer time will be protected, guarded, and covered with the blood of Christ and angelic servants.

I bind the demonic realm from hearing my prayers and prophecies and activating against them, in Jesus' name.

I call forth the Spirit of the living God to saturate this meeting with His presence and His love, in Jesus' name!

I bless You, Lord, for what You are going to do here today, and I invite You Holy Spirit to come in and have your way. Come in and teach, instruct, and discipline today.

Kingdom Faith

I declare and decree my faith will be daily exhibited.

I proclaim I am a servant to the King.

I call forth the love and power of God to be released to all I come in contact with.

The resurrection power of Jesus lives in me to pray for healing and see it manifest!

The love of God permeates me!

His Word is my identity!

I am one with the Word, and the Word is one with me!

The Kingdom manifests out of me every moment!

I am overflowing with the joy of the Lord!

I am energized and strengthened to walk in the anointing all the time!

I am about My Father's business, which is Kingdom business.

Life flows from me, abundantly!

I lovingly serve the Lord and people with excess from the throne of God.

We can prophesy and speak and decree over our lives. We do not need to wait for a prophet to speak over us when we can hear clearly from the Lord. Every year I encourage the people who receive from my teaching to write a prophetic word over themselves for the year. On these pages, write a prophetic proclamation prophesying over yourself and what you desire to see happen in your life.

_____

_____

_____

_____

_____

_____

_____

_____

_____

_____

_____

_____

_____

_____

_____

_____

_____

_____

_____

_____

_____

_____

_____

_____

_____

_____

_____

_____

_____

_____

_____

_____

_____

_____

_____•

Infertility

I command my body to be fruitful and multiply, according to the Word of God.

I call forth eggs to release on a timely basis and connect with sperm.

I call forth my uterus to work properly, in Jesus' name.

I proclaim infertility, delay, and lack of conception to leave, in Jesus' name.

My bloodline and the bloodline of my children are covered in the blood of Jesus.

I command children to be produced from my womb.

I thank You, Lord, You fearfully and wonderfully made me in my mother's womb, and I command that miracle-working power to go throughout my womb right now. Womb produce life, be fertile, in Jesus' name.

I command man parts to be strong and work properly. Sperm, produce abundantly, be strong, get to your destination, in Jesus' name.

I call forth divine intervention in my womb. I am redeemed from the curse.

I thank You, Father, You created life and designed life for my womb.

My womb is strong and healthy and can carry several children to full term.

God, as You opened Rachel's womb, I speak to my womb, and I say be opened by the power of God.

God's Word says the fruit of my womb will be blessed. Womb, produce fruit and life, abundantly, in Jesus' name.

I come against the enemy and say, "You will not destroy the destiny of any future child of mine. You will not destroy my marriage by having dissension and irritation through infertility."

I will have no miscarriages or premature deaths of my children, in Jesus' name!

No weapon formed against my womb and childbearing will prosper!

I call forth life in abundance and that my children will serve the Lord all the days of their lives, in Jesus' powerful, mighty name.

Physical Healing

I decree and declare health and healing to come into my body right now!

I live in divine health!

I am life, because Jesus is life, and Jesus lives in me!

Sickness and disease can not and will not live in my body!

I have been given a blood transfusion, and the blood of Jesus exists in my veins and is running to every tissue and organ producing life and health.

I will live by my heavenly Father's Word and not by a doctor's report.

I come against doctor's reports, and in the mighty name of Jesus, I speak against any diagnosis given that does not line up with the Word of God.

I claim the scriptures that Christ heals all and every time and I call forth that divine healing He purchased on the cross for me.

I rebuke the devourer and call my body into the light of God's love.

I claim I am healed, whole, delivered, and set free from any and all physical infirmity.

The blood of Jesus runs through my veins.

I am equipped for every good work of the Lord.

I live in victory.

I live healed!

Jesus healed the sick. Throughout the Gospels, we read stories of how He brought forth the ministry of healing and deliverance. Speaking to our body parts and telling them to come into alignment with the Word of God and to manifest their healing is powerful. Write your own healing declarations based on scriptural facts and telling those organs to work in the perfection God created them. Command your physical ailments to be reversed and for health to manifest in your body.

_____

_____

_____

_____

_____

_____

_____

_____

_____

_____

_____

_____

Financial
Pastor Ron DeGraw

I sow my financial seed into the Kingdom.

I declare and decree that I am no longer under the curse.

I sow my seed in faith and in the promises of God.

I declare freedom from the World's economy and lack.

I speak the word of faith over my seed that, as I walk according to the Word and obey God's Word, He will make my way prosperous, and I will have good success.

I say that everything I do will prosper.

I thank You, Lord, that You have blessed me so that I can be a blessing to others.

I claim this seed to be prosperous, and as I sow, I will increase even more.

I speak this all in Jesus' name.

Home Sale Declaration

I call forth the perfect buyers for my house.

Lord, have the buyers for my house put their house on the market.

I command the finances to come forth for the buyers of my home.

I dispatch angels on assignment to sell my home.

Expose and highlight my house on the listings.

I call forth my realtor to work on my behalf.

I command my house to sell for full market price or above.

I cover the sale and transaction with the blood of Christ.

The Bible speaks frequently about finances. God desires us to live in prosperity. Write a proclamation claiming and decreeing that your debts are paid in full, that you are debt-free. Command your checking and savings accounts to increase. Speak to your paycheck and tell your salary to increase.

My Financial Declaration

_____

_____

_____

_____

_____

_____

_____

_____

_____

_____

_____

_____

_____

_____●

Lack of finances and debt hold people in bondage and poverty and lack mentality.

Write a proclamation to change your mind and way of thinking and call forth that you are a giver.

_____

_____

_____

_____

_____

_____

_____

_____

_____

_____

_____

_____

_____

_____

_____

My **financial** declaration changing my way of thinking when it comes to finances.

_____

_____
_____
_____
_____
_____
_____
_____
_____
_____
_____
_____
_____
_____
_____
_____
_____

_____●

My **Financial** declaration calling forth that I am a giver!

_____

_____

_____

_____

_____

_____

_____

_____

_____

_____

_____

_____

_____

_____

_____

_____

_____

_____

_____

Powerful Prophetic Saturation

I call forth the love of God to manifest in me.

Overwhelm me, Lord, with Your presence and love. Let me experience You!

I call forth a saturation of His presence to permeate my life, home, and workplace.

I proclaim He will use me as a mighty vessel overflowing with the goodness of His pleasure.

I say everything I do will prosper. God's Word will be sent forth in my life.

I command the heaven's to open and angels to activate and be dispatched on my behalf.

I order and instruct a fresh heavenly rain to fall upon me, drawing me into a place of shalom and tranquility with Him.

I establish God's order in my life and command all chaos to dissipate, in Jesus' name.

I proclaim this will be a day established in the Lord that

I will remember where change manifested, freedom occurred, and the opportunities God has written for me will manifest.

I seal this prophetic decree in and call it forth for my life today in the name of Jesus, by the blood of the Lamb, and in the power and love of our Father God!

Releasing the Past

I am moving forward!

I leave behind old habits and patterns.

I break agreement with offense, anger, and rejection in my life!

All ungodly soul ties and relationships will no longer affect me.

I am no longer a victim, but I am victorious!

Provision for my destiny, come forth!

Divine connections for ministry appointments, manifest!

My mind is full of truth, and no lies of the enemy will infiltrate it!

I speak the Word of God, life, and health into my body.

I am healed by His stripes.

I am a giver and will have more than enough to disperse.

I will saturate others in God's love at all times.

My dreams and desires will come forth!

I will gain much spiritual growth.

Favor, blessing, and abundance are mine, in Jesus' name!

Prophetic Fulfillment, Come Forth

I call forth every vision and prophetic fulfillment according to the Word of God for my life, in Jesus' name.

I command the Word of God to come forth for my life, my family, and my finances. My ministry is to be delayed no longer, in Jesus' name.

The word which the Lord has spoken to me shall come to pass, no more postponed in Jesus' name.

The Lord says the word and performs it over my life, in Jesus' name.

I decree none of God's words or plans for my life will be postponed any longer, in Jesus' name.

Spirit of God, send forth Your plans and purposes for my life today, in Jesus' name.

I call forth the fulfillment of every Godly vision I've had. I proclaim this is my time, and season for an increase.

The Lord says His word and performs it. The Lord is performing His word on my behalf.

My visions and my prophecies are coming to pass.

Spiritual realm, hear the word of the Lord spoken and activate on my behalf, in Jesus' name.

Victorious

I proclaim I am victorious!

I decree everywhere I step I shall be prosperous and victorious.

I declare I am victorious over my enemies.

I decree and declare I am victorious in my business and ministry.

No weapon formed against me shall prosper, I am victorious.

I bind and rebuke curses. They shall not rise against me. I am victorious.

Emotional bondage does not plague me. I shall be victorious.

I do not manifest intimidation. I am victorious.

I declare and decree health and healing to come into my body.

I say declarations and decrees come forth easily and with precision.

I speak to the dry bones and dead areas of my life to come to life and come forth that are according to the will of God.

Unfruitfulness and unproductivity that distracts me, be removed according to God's will.

I call forth ministry connections and appointments to come forth speedily and with confirmation according to God's will.

I declare the mountains and obstacles in my life to crumble, in Jesus' name.

We are conquerors and victorious. We have an inheritance in heaven! Our identity is in Christ.

Write a proclamation claiming all that you are and all that you want to be.

_____

_____

_____

_____

_____

_____

_____

_____

_____

_____

_____

_____

_____

_____

_____

_____

_____

Protection

I proclaim the devil and his cohorts will be under my feet as it is stated in the Bible.

I say I will rise up and take the authority Jesus gave to me.

No worry, no fear, no doubt, and no burden bearing will attack or plague me, in Jesus' name.

My health and the health of my family will be perfect and complete. Our bodies will not malfunction. They will produce abundant life.

I command business ideas, investments, and a mind of entrepreneurship to come forth. I thank You, God, creative ideas are coming my way.

I plead the blood of Jesus over my family, team, ministries, and children.

I call forth my children and my spouse to fall more in love with you, Jesus, and to serve the Lord all the days of their life, in Jesus' name.

I say this year I will eat healthily and my body will lose fat.

I call forth the glory of the Lord to be established and released in those I love and throughout the Earth.

I say and commit to doing my part this year to desecrate racism.

My mind and my thoughts will be complete in Him, lacking nothing. My mind will not wander or stray with vain imaginations but will be continually focused on Him and His goodness.

I claim this will be a year that my storehouses will overflow.

I call forth this year will be a fruitful year for the Kingdom and that my tree will yield much fruit.

I call forth the vault of heaven to open on my behalf. May the vault of revelation be open to me to feast from.

I proclaim this will be a year that the past sins in my mind will truly be erased.

May the abundance of heaven drop on me like dewdrops of rain.

I purpose and plan to study the Word of God daily and to allow it to ignite me.

I originate from God, and since I have His DNA, I will act like Him.

Every dark path in my life will now shine with the light of God.

I pronounce this to be a year of release of good things in my life and ministry in the name of Jesus.

Worship

I proclaim and announce this will be a day of worship to the King.

I call forth the glory of God to descend while I worship.

I say I will worship in freedom and truth without distractions!

I bind distractions from entering and plaguing my worship time.

My worship time will be holy and pure, not infected with unclean thoughts.

I thank You, Lord, that I can approach Your throne of grace and receive mercy in the time of need.

Lord, let my praises be sweet to You.

I will bless the Lord at all times.

I thank You, Lord, I have energy and strength in my body.

I claim new revelation will come forth while I worship.

I call forth intimacy with the Father, communion with Him while I lift my hands in praise and adoration to the King.

About the Author

Kathy DeGraw is a prophetic spiritual warfare and deliverance minister releasing the love and power of God, to ignite and activate people, release prophetic destinies and deliver people from the bondage of the enemy. She is the founder of Kathy De-Graw Ministries and travels internationally preaching at conference events and empowering and discipling people through her teaching schools.

She writes weekly for *Charisma* online magazine and hosts a weekly Prophetic Spiritual Warfare show on the Charisma Podcast Network. She is a recognized prophetic voice on The Elijah List, Destiny Image and Prophecy Investigators. She has authored several books, including *Discerning and Destroying the Works of Satan, Speak Out,* and *Warfare Declarations.*

She is the founder of Ruach Ha'Kodesh Apostolic Empowerment Center, which she co-pastors with her husband, Be Love Outreach, a local outreach hosting evangelistic events and prophetic love tours and Change Into Colorless, an anti-racism corporation.

Kathy is married to her husband, Pastor Ron DeGraw; they reside in Grandville, Michigan, and they have three young adult children, Dillon, Amber, and Lauren (and son-in-law, Alex) who all serve the Lord and reside in Grandville, Michigan.

To inquire with Kathy
for a Ministry Event, contact:
Kathy DeGraw Ministries
P.O. Box 65 • Grandville, Michigan 49468
Website: www.kathydegrawministries.org
Email: admin@degrawministries.org

•

Follow Kathy
on
Facebook,
YouTube
and
Instagram
@ Kathy DeGraw

Additional Books
by Kathy DeGraw

Unshackled
[Chosen Books]

Discerning and Destroying the Works of Satan
[Destiny Image]

Speak Out
[Creation House]

A Worship-Woven Life: Learning to Live a Life of Praise
[Tate Publishing]

The Sky's the Limit: Creating an Amazing Kids' CLub
[CSS Publishing]

Warfare Declarations
Baptism of Fire and Power
[K Publishing]

Why Christians Shouldn't Celebrate Halloween
[Charisma Media]

Reasons of captivity

I seat myself in Heavenly places
I see myself there + dancing
w/ the father.

I pull myself up from Jezebel/
Python Spirit + Leviathan
Spirit go.
I call truth to my mind,
my life now.
Mind binding spirits you have
no power over me, you go
Every spirit holding my
destiny + real self + real personality
back you must go.
Complacency & passivity demons
you must go.
I command my flesh to not
agree or operate in passivity
or complacency anymore.
I call back my
childhood
I call back my
life, I call back my joy,
my creativity
my freedom
from the prison of captivity

Made in the USA
Monee, IL
17 July 2022